INTRODUCTION TO THE AGILE PROJECT MANAGER

Clarisse Genbers

Contents

Chapter One

Introduction to Agile Project Management Method

In management, everyone manages projects. Whether you are a certified manager or not, at some point they had to manage their projects to ensure that the delivered final product met the customer's requirements. Unfortunately, most managers manage their projects by "holding on". This often results in difficulties in effectively managing multiple projects simultaneously or meeting deadlines, as well as adapting to ever-changing project requirements. In an effort to solve the project management challenges that most people face, companies use several standard project management methodologies .In regards to the above, the best way to mitigate the challenges associated with project management is to adopt a project management technique that works. However, given the many methods available, choosing one becomes a daunting task. Most people would struggle to determine the best method for them. Fortunately, this book will walk you through the agile project management methodology as one of the best strategies you can use to manage your projects.So what is agility? Agile refers to project management techniques that use short development cycles called "sprints" to focus on continuous improvement when developing a product or service. Basically, agile is a method used to manage projects. This project management method can be used for any project management process. However, it was actually set up to assist in software develop ment.In the past, industries used conventional approaches to manage their projects. During this time, companies have been using methods like the one earnedvalue management or the PERT method to coordinate project activities. As global economies changed, there was a shift in focus on what needed to be delivered to the end customer. In the past, the importance of quality and doing good was a great emphasis. With the changing times, new management techniques have developed. Doing things right was no longer enough. Businesses now have to learn how to get things done on time. Without a doubt, the desire of customers to receive their products or services on time has changed the way companies do business. Unfortunately, if a company fails to meet the timely demands of its customers, its competitors in the market will respond as needed. However, project managers in companies need to wake up and appreciate the changes around them. In other words, they need to become more agile.The advent of the Internet has also brought changes, especially in the way companies handle project management activities. Today, companies must embrace the importance of using project management methods such as agile. The term 'agile' is defined as 'being able to move quickly and easily'. From this definition, project managers are expected to quickly adapt to their changing environment. In this case, they must quickly adapt to changing customer needs.The advent of the Internet has led to numerous uncertainties in project management. Most project managers will agree that it is nearly impossible to keep track of all changes in a project management process. After starting a project, a client realizes that he didn't want exactly what he originally asked for. Unfortunately, the cost to any organization of such rapid change is immense. This is especially true when projects are not completed on time or when the final product or service does not meet consumer needs. An approach that aspiresDealing with such unpredictability while recognizing the importance of learning in the project life cycle should therefore be used in every organization. This approach is called “agile project management.”

Chapter Two

History of Agile

As mentioned rather, agile project management was initially developed as a way to aid in software development. In the early 1990s, when PC computing began to take shape in most industries, software development went through a major crisis. During this period, the crisis was referred to as "application delivery delay". As the name suggests, the industry faced a major problem to deliver software in a short amount of time. The time it took a company to produce its actual application was about three ye ars.The problem was that companies were moving faster than application development. This then led to a scenario where projects could be canceled as they were no longer needed due to the delay. As a result of the failures, people became frustrated with the process. Jon Kern, an aerospace engineer in the 1990s, was deeply disappointed in the process. Over time, Kern and other software development leaders have pushed for better software development processes.As a result of their proposals, there have been major changes. For example, it took the auto industry about six years to design a new car. In the 1990s, this time was reduced to almost half of the initial time. Given the frustrations surrounding unproductive software development activities, this led to the notable Snowbirds reunion held in Utah in 2001. This was the second time this group had reunited after their first reunion in 2000. At their conference, agility was not their primary focus. At the time, other terms were also used to refer to the practice, including "light" and "light".The primary goal of software thought leaders was to rapidly develop software and put it in the hands of consumers. There were numerous benefits associated with such fast software delivery. Users were able to enjoy the benefits of the software much faster. The software development team also benefited from the rapid feedback on the functionality of the software.It was through the benefits such as quick feedback and the general willingness to change that were the most important aspects of agile movement.

Chapter Three

Advantages of Agile Project Management

With When it comes to project management, there are numerous benefits that project teams, project leaders, sponsors, and customers gain from using Agile. To clearly understand how agility is beneficial to project management, it is essential to understand what is meant by the term "project management". The process of managing a project is a challenging task when a company does not know all the areas in which it has to work. For a project to be successful, it depends on the individual parts being assembled to function optimally. One of the main reasons why projects fail is the misalignment between the business strategy and the project objectives. A project can also fail due to a lack of administrative support or sponsorship. Likewise, it can fail due to vague existing business goals and requirements. These are just some of the reasons why most projects fail.For a project to be successful, it is necessary to identify the essential people, processes, techniques and technologies necessary for success. With this in mind, project management is defined as the union of processes, skills, knowledge, techniques and inputs and outputs used by project managers to complete a project.S ome of the basic objectives of project management that every strategic body should pursue:• Create a picture that shows that the PMO and EPMO are aligned with the company's goals. • Provide senior managers with valuable information.• Get the right people, the right knowledge and skills.• Report on key areas of interest to the company.• Identification of PMO and EPMO performance.Successful project management requires more than just an individual's technical know-how. There are also other non-technical skills that good managers should represent. An ideal project manager should possess soft skills such as leadership, communication, prioritization, organization, problem solving, adaptability and mo tivation.It is also worth noting that the project management process is broken down into five distinct stages, including:• Initiation• Plans• Run• Monitor and control• ClosingApplying the agile project management method to any project management task has many benefits. Some of them are discussed belo w.Improved product qualityThe use of agile project management ensures the improvement of the final quality of any product or service. It is worth noting that agile supports the idea of testing a product at every stage of its life cycle. This means that there are regular checks to make sure the product is also being used during thestages of development. In line with this, the product owner can easily make the necessary changes to the product. The result is a product that meets customer needs in every corner. Agile methods offer ideal protection against product problems. Therefore, the agile method promotes a proactive approach to avoid product-related complications. Likewise, agile embraces technological excellence and sustainable development as part of producing a quality product that meets customer needs. The agile methodology helps the management team define and process requirements quickly enough to ensure that product features are relevant to customer expectations.During the development process, a product also goes through daily testing and continuous integration. As a result, the development team is in a better position to address product issues while they are still fresh. This helps immensely as there are little or no delays if there are any changes or issues that need to be addressed. Higher Customer Satisfaction

Using the agile method also leads to greater customer satisfaction. This is easy to achieve because the product owner is fully involved in the product development process. The Product Owner is better acquainted with the product requirements and customer expectations. Keeping them busy therefore ensures that the final product meets the customer's needs. Ultimately, consumers are more likely to be satisfied with the delivered product. In addition to involving the product owner, the agile method also involves the customer throughout the project. This means that there is a good chance that the product contains what the customer wants. Greater customer satisfaction is also achieved by ensuring the product backlogconstantly prioritized and updated to help product developers respond quickly to ch anges.Customers are also regularly informed about the functionality of the product during each stage of the development process. Of course, this also helps minimize last-minute changes, which often impact the delivery of the final product. Ultimately, the agile method allows a product to be delivered quickly enough to capitalize on existing market demand. With these changes through the application of the agile method, customers are not only satisfied with the timely delivery of products, but also with the quality of products they receive in the market .Improved team moraleThe idea of working with a self-organizing team creates a working environment where people are innovative and creative. The best part is that the individuals are also recognized for their expertise. Regarding this advantage, a project manager is there to remove existing obstacles in the development team. As such, there would be no outside interference. Keeping in mind that there are several functional areas that all have the same goal, these people will learn new skills. Over time, they can improve their skills by learning from other people on the team.More collaborationThe cross-functional team according to the agile method regularly works closely together. Scrum meetings held daily allow the development team to effectively organize work by planning future assignments and addressing development roadblocks. The Scrum Master, Product Owner, and development team also communicate regularly with stakeholders during sprint reviews. This promotes better cooperation between all parties involved in product development.More relevant statisticsIf we compare the metrics used by agile project teams with those used conventionally, the metrics used by agile project teams are more accurate and relevant. In most cases, these metrics help to inaccurately estimate project time, project cost, and overall performance. This also leads to better decisions. Improved performance visibilityThe best thing about agile projects is that team members have the ability to understand how the project is progressing at each stage. This can be done through daily sprint reviews and daily Scrum meetings. Visible graphs are also provided as a concrete way to see the progress of the project. Therefore, there is better performance visibility. Nobody is left in the dark during the product development process. Increased project controlUsing agile project management creates many opportunities for the team to constantly review the project. This means that team members have a better opportunity to exercise control over the project in addition to regular sprint meetings. The fact that every member of the team is informed of the progress of the project means that there is transparency on how things are done.Improved project predictabilityIn addition to improved project control, project predictability is also enhanced through the many tools and practices used by the project team. For example, it is possible to predict how much the project will cost and how long it will take to complete it. The information gained from daily Scrum meetings helps the team easily predict the likely performance of the product in the market.Reduced riskThe use of agile methods ensures that the risks of absolute project failure are eliminated. The idea is to have a functional product from the first sprint. Developing a product in sprints ensures that the whole project never completely fails. If there's something to change, it's easy to do by sorting into a specific sprint rather than scrapping the whole project. In addition, the project is adapted to the customer's requirements at each stage of development. This implies that usable functions are integrated to ensure the relevance of the product to be developed. This minimizes the probability of project failure.There are also self-funded projects that are used to generate income at an early stage. Therefore, organizations can finance a project with low initial costs. The idea that a project will fail due to lack of funds is eliminated.Faster ROIThe advantages of a product under development can be experienced already during the development phases. This means that the organization can easily see a quick return on investment (ROI). Agile means that a product is quickly brought to market. Therefore, if customers request changes, they can be made quickly. The advantage is that an organization using Agile gains a competitive advantage over other companies fighting for the same market.There is a good reason why organizations should use this method to manage their projects. The fact that a product is delivered to market faster means that time-to-market is also fast and efficient. The agile project team is productive. The organization then has the opportunity to do sogain a competitive advantage over competitors in the market. Agile project management leads to better product quality delivered to the market.

Chapter Four

The Main Principles of Agile Project Management

A deeper A look at agile management shows that there are principles that govern the management of a project. In other words, it says a lot about how an agile project should be managed. There are 12 principles of agile project management.1. The highest priority is to meet customer requirements through timely and continuous delivery. 2. Changes are recognized at every stage of product development.3. There is a higher frequency of delivery of the product or service.4. Stakeholders and developers work closely together during product or service development.5. The project is built around a group of motivated people.6. Face-to-face interactions are considered the most effective form of communication. 7. A working product is the most important measure of success.8. Agile processes promote sustainable development.9. Agility is enhanced by continuous attention to detail, good design and excellence.10. Simplicity is key.11. The use of self-organizing teams leads to the development of ideal architectures and designs that help meet requirements. 12. Regular intervals are used to inspect and adjust to ensure effectiveness.A look at these principles shows that the principles serve as a guideline for how different people can work together and work towards a common goal. There are many topics that touch on these principles, including interpersonal interactions, managerial behavior, team behavior, continuous improvement, and measuring progress. More information on the principles of agile project management is discussed below chapter.

Chapter Five

Understand the Principles of Agile Project Management

Generally, The best way to understand what agility is is that it is a way of managing projects. Well, the method was first introduced to aid in software development. And Agile can be used in any organization. Companies often have to carry out projects that provide products and services to their customers. In order to ensure that these projects run smoothly, people need to interact with each other in the best way possible. The team working on the project must also work together effectively. More importantly, the progress of the project should be constantly monitored to get the best performance. The agile method helps to achieve all this. This method governs how a project is managed. The 12 principles of agile project management are discussed in detail here. client satisfactionThe first principle of the agile method is customer satisfaction. A project manager's goal should be to deliver a problem-solving product or service. Customer satisfaction is achieved not only by delivering quality products, but also by delivering the product on time and ensuring that the continuous delivery of the product is maintained. This therefore requires minimizing the time spent at each stage of product development. The project manager must work to make the development process more efficient. Implementing the agile method ensures that unnecessary activities are reduced in order to meet customer requirements.Make and manage changesOne of the biggest benefits of the agile project management method is that it gives the project manager the flexibility they need in terms of changes. Compared to other project management methods, it can be difficult to make changes depending on the development phase of the project. For example, it would be difficult to make the necessary changes in the later stages of development. However, the agile project management method makes this possible. How can the agile method help bring about changes even in the later stages of the project development cycle? Well, customers change their minds all the time. New technologies may come to market and customers expect this technology to be incorporated into the product. Therefore, you must adapt accordingly. That's agility. If you decided to launch a product and ignore customer requests, it could be a waste of money. You would end up releasing obsolete technology. By using the agile project management method, you can efficiently make changes that ensure the released product meets the client's wishes. Agile can help manage change throughout the product development process in several way s.Continuous customer entryA major advantage of the agile method is that it allows for customer input at every stage of product development. Therefore, the development team can use customer feedback sooner rather than later. If the customer wants new features, they are considered and changes are made immediately.Priorities established via Product BacklogThe agile methodology fosters a collaborative environment where customers and the entire project development team can provide input on what should be prioritized. The ability for all members to add anything to the product backlog is an ideal way to make changes and prioritize.Effective communication through daily meetingsIdeally, the best way to manage frequent changes during the product development process is to hold daily meetings around the same time. The importance of these meetings is that the members have the opportunity to discuss the tasks related to the project. This means that they can also talk about existing obstacles and ways to overcome them.These meetings can be very helpful in discussing product needs. Regular discussions can help to cope with changes in a very short time.Task processing by task boardsTraditionally, the project team knows the product requirements by reading the requirements documents. These documents are often overlooked as they are simply read once and left in the mailbox. With Agile, tasks are distributed via a task board. This table divides the tasks into different columns and they are visible 24/7. The visibility gained through the use of the task board makes it easy to change requirements.Making and managing change is part of all project requirements. A development team should have a plan for how to resolve these changes. The agile method offers the project development team an ideal platform to deal with these changes. Ultimately, effective change brings a product to market that meets customer n eeds.Shorter time scaleThe third principle of agile project management relates to the idea of delivering a product in less time. In the past, the product development process was mostly occupied with documentation. For example, in software development, a lot of emphasis has been placed on paperwork. There was a lot of documentation for which nothing to show. On the contrary, the agile method places a lot of emphasis on reducing delivery times. The focus is on product development rather than just planning.

Chapter Six

Working Together

Principle number four states that stakeholders and developers work closely together during product or service development. This principle calls for a collaborative environment in which individual members understand that they are working towards a common goal. When employees work in remote offices, project managers must use the best tools to facilitate communication. Teams need to work together to exchange ideas and understand each other. Greater productivity is achieved by working together. Working with a group of motivated people-Several people are working to achieve the goal of the project. One of the most important questions to ask yourself as a project manager is: "Why did you hire them?" Sure, you hired your team because of their qualifications. This means you have to let them do what they do best. Don't micromanage. Micromanagement only drives the talent pool. Working with the right team is crucial. Therefore, you should have done a thorough check beforehand. It means you trust your team members to deliver.Project Managers or Scrum Masters should do their best to provide the support the team needs. They should also regularly monitor what the team is doing to ensure they are following the necessary guidelines. The important thing here is that the team needs to have the perception that you trust them to perform.Face-to-face communicationSimply put, a project manager should strive to shorten the time to get answers to her questions. Therefore, the way of communicating face to face is considered an ideal form. The agile management method requires people to work together in an environment where they can easily have face-to-face interactions. However, this does not mean that advanced communication methods should not be used. In addition to supporting face-to-face interaction, the project manager must incorporate the use of advanced communication tools. If there are employees in remote locations, video calling is essential. It's about creating a more collaborative communication environment .Does the product work?The main measure of the success of the project is whether the product works. When you develop software, success is measured by whether the software is up and running. Ideally, your success will not be measured by ticking off tasks; It's only part of the process. However, the success of the project will be measured by the functionality of the product. In other words, the purpose of the project is not to go through the process from beginning to end. If the product doesn't work, all your efforts count for nothing. Other factors that led to the completion of the project are irrelevant if the final product does not work.Sustainable developmentThe main reason why short activity sprints are highly recommended in the agile methodology is not only to make quick changes, but also to keep the team motivated. Often people suffer from burnout by doing similar activities over a long period of time. It's normal. To avoid this, the agile methodology advocates short productive bursts. Working on a specific activity for a short period of time leads to increased productivity. The project manager must set the right pace for accomplishing small activities. The project team must be satisfied with its achievements.Continuous improvementA project manager must always ensure that the product he is working on is constantly being improved. Whether you're working on code or something more concrete, it's important to recognize that improvements can be seen at every step or step. The last thing to do is to come back later to fix things that happened to you before. If you need to fix the problems, fix them now. The goal is not to go back to cleaning. Make any necessary changes as you progress. This saves a lot of time and ensures that the product is delivered on time. Simplicity is keySimplicity is the key to delivering a product in the shortest possible time. This means that your role as a project manager is to remove the complexities. Team members should not waste their time trying to understand the process. Make it easy for them to complete it on time. The good news is that the process can be simplified with the project management tools at your disposal. So make sure your team doesn't focus on what's not important to ensure a project is completed successfully. Don't forget to use management tools to automate the process.Self-organized teamsThe best way to know if your team is agile enough is to measure whether it is self-steering. A great team must take the lead without being pushed. If you find yourself micromanaging the team, this is a red flag. The individual teams you work with must do what needs to be done. They must be present to solve problems and propose ideal solutions. A project manager should only step in when difficult problems arise or step in when something is wrong that needs to be addressed quickly. In normal situations, everything should work smoothly. The credit does not go to the project manager but to the self-organizing teams. Inspect and adjustInspection and customization are another essential principle to adopt in agile project management. Throughout the development process, the team should stop regularly and explore what can be done to make things better. If something needs to be adjusted, it should be done immediately. By adjusting here and there there is a guarantee that the project will be successful.Adheri ng to the 12 principles of agile project management is essential to the success of any project. Regardless of the project you are working on, with these principles you will realize that it is easy to deliver a product in a certain amount of time. Most importantly, reduce common productivity risks while managing project costs effectively. Easy said; increase your chances of success in your project management activities.

Chapter Seven

The importance

The application of the agile project management method aims to increase the chances of project success. In this case, your team's agility keeps the team productive over a longer period of time. From the information discussed in the previous chapter, it is clear that there are many advantages associated with the agile management method. At first glance, these benefits seem easy to obtain. However, it should be noted that not all projects benefit from applying the agile project management method. To ensure that you are effectively applying agility to your project management, it is essential to understand if the method is right for you. Adopting the Agile method means that your organization changes from the way it worked before. Agility requires a quick approach. Everything must be clarified beforehand.Therefore, it is vital for your business to determine whether it is up to scratch or not. To find out, you need to answer the following questions:• Are you willing to start projects without knowing the result?By applying the agile project management method, you need to act quickly. The method promotes the idea of acting quickly and consistently by conducting tests during the product development process. This is not easy. It is stressful if not managed effectively. So, are you ready to take on the challenge?Before adopting the agile method, consider whether you are willing to test your product before it is completed. It is essential to be prepared to test the cake before it is fully cooked.• How careful are you about risks?Applying the agile project development method means taking more risks than the traditional way of doing things. When using this method, you should embrace the idea of learning from your mistakes while striving to deliver a product that meets customer needs. However, take a step back to assess whether you can handle the risk. To follow the Agile path, you must be prepared for unknown problems or risks that may arise during product development.• Do you have an agile team?Determine if your team is agile enough to handle project needs. Remember that one of the principles of the agile method is that it insists on a more collaborative environment. As such, your team should be ready to work together towards a common goal. Team members need to put aside their differences and work together harmoniously. Undeniably, if your team isn't agile enough, the agile project management method won't be as effective as it could be.If you're happy with the answers to these questions, you're ready to change the way your business works. The following section will guide you step by step in applying the agile project management method to your business activities. The complete guide in this section will help you learn how to develop your products in an agile way.Step 1: Define your vision in a strategy meetingThe first thing to address in the early stages of the agile project is your vision. What should your project solve? That's the big picture of what you want to do. It gives your team a purpose and a mission. Product companies can better articulate their visions through the elevator pitch. This concept defines your target customers. It should also say something about the need the project will address. In particular, the main advantage of using the set of products to be launched or introduced should also be considered. In other words, what is the compelling reason that would motivate people to buy the product?Some people need to be present during this phase of the agile project. Key stakeholders include managers, directors and other executives as well as product owners.When should you define your vision? Basically, the meeting must take place before the start of a project. When a project is underway, a strategy meeting could also be organized to ensure that all members are aware of existing updates.

Step 2: Develop a Product Roadmap

After in devising a vision, the product owner must translate the vision into a roadmap. This is a visual summary that maps the vision and direction of product development. It acts as a plan to be used in the execution of the strategy. Note that the roadmap uses a separate time frame. This means that the planning process is not just about defining each step. Instead, the roadmap identifies and prioritizes the effort required to deliver a usable pro duct.The best roadmap is focused. Formulation of a roadmap should be done by the Product Owner, but input from other stakeholders is also welcome. For example, development, marketing, support and sales representatives should be consulted. The process of creating a roadmap should be done right after the strategy meeting. Step 3: Create a release planOnce you have developed a work strategy and plan that will help you achieve your goals, the next step is to create a calendar. This is where the release plan comes in handy. During this phase, the Product Owner creates a high-level calendar that is used for the release of a working product. You have to realize that agile projects will have multiple versions. Features must be prioritized to make sure you can get started at any time. The schedule must take into account the complexity of the project and the duration of the sprints. All team members must be present during the posting schedule. During this stage, team members will be energized and ready to take on the challenge ahead.Step 4: Sprint PlanningThe first steps described here show the macro view of the agile project development phase. The sprint planning stage is a micro view as it takes into account the specific tasks that will be performed to develop the product. Usually, an ideal sprint lasts from one to four weeks. The sprint duration should be the same throughout the development process. The importance of an equal sprint duration is that it allows team members to effectively plan how future work will be handled based on past performance.At the start of the sprint cycle, the project manager and other team members must submit a short list of backlog items that must be completed within the allotted sprint time.All team members must be present during the planning phase of the sprint. Their contributions will make a huge difference in developing a product tailored to customer needs.Step 5: hold daily meetingsDaily meetings work closely with the daily sprints you do. The project manager will organize daily meetings to discuss what was completed the previous day. During these meetings, any existing roadblocks are drawn. Usually the daily meeting lasts about 15 minutes. In addition to discussing what was completed yesterday, the team also talks about what needs to be done today and the existing obstacles that prevent them from achieving their goals.Each team member must understand the importance of holding regular meetings. Agile project management is all about speed. This can only be achieved through regular monitoring of the progress of the project. The daily meetings allow you to identify areas for improvement and work on issues that could be an obstacle.

Step

6:

Sprint

Review

Assuming that everything goes according to plan during the sprint cycles, your team should have a working product at this stage. If you are developing software, the software should work once you get to this step. At this point, team members need to review what they have already done.The review process must be followed by the interested parties as they have to see the work of the product. Essentially this is where you show off and say more about the product. The importance of this step is that all team members sit together to determine if the requirements have been met in the development stages. The product owner can accept or decline certain features included in the product. If there are any errors, the team can discuss ways to fix them in the next sprint. Agility is about learning and correcting mistakes in each sprint cycle. It is worth pointing out that sprint evaluation should be done after each sprint. Therefore, the team cannot go into another sprint without revisiting the first one.Step 7: Sprint RetrospectiveIn this step, team members discuss how the previous sprint went and also take time to discuss how the next sprint should be improved. The idea of agile project management is not just about planning. He also strives to ensure that the progress of a project is well monitored and improved throughout the development process. The advantage is that changes can easily be made, even at advanced stages of development. Like the sprint review, the sprint retrospective should be performed after each sprint.After this step, the product owner should have a working product. You can launch the product at any time and get feedback from your customers as you make changes. The continuous process of delivering a product without actually completing it completely is what makes the agile method powerful. You don't have to work on a product all year round and release it only to find that some aspects of core functionality are missing. It could be devastating because you would have to start the whole processproduct development again. The agile method helps you develop and follow the product in sprints until it meets customer expec tations.Step 8: Make Mistakes and ImproveAt the end of each sprint, you should collect feedback and find ideal opportunities for improvement. Making mistakes should not be taken negatively. On the contrary, the group should learn from its mistakes and adapt accordingly. Sprint review and sprint retrospective steps should identify these errors. Then the team works together to propose solutions to address the errors.Step 9: matureRegular inspection and learning from mistakes will help the team grow and mature. They will learn a lot from the mistakes of the past. Therefore, they will be able to more easily evade challenges in future projects and there will be improvement from one sprint exercise to the next. Think of it this way: big companies like Microsoft and Google can update their products every week using the agile method. For this reason, they remind you of their regular product updates. Simply stated; Their products evolve with constant improvements adapted to the needs of customers. They remain the best on the market because they use the agile project management method. Keep this in mind when considering bringing agility to your business team.

Chapter Eight

Setting Up Your Own Agile Environment and the Team Composition

After To understand how to apply the agile method in your organization, it is essential to understand how to use it. The environment in which your team works must be sufficiently agile to guarantee the achievement of the objectives set. As already mentioned, agility here refers to the speed at which an organization adapts to changes. The work environment should be conducive to an agile workplace. This section walks you through the steps of creating an agile environment. We also take a closer look at the composition of an agile team.What is an Agile environment?What does it mean to work in an agile environment? This refers to an environment that creates and nurtures a culture to motivate a team of individuals to work in harmony towards a common goal. Great value is placed on the interactions of these individuals and their abilities. An agile organization can be distinguished from any other organization that uses traditional project management strategies. Some characteristics of agile organizations can help to understand what an agile environment should be. The common characteristics of an agile environment are briefly described bel ow.Leadership is about purposeAgile environments strive to shorten the distance between developing a product and delivering it to the end user. Therefore, leadership in an agile environment places more emphasis on the mission objective than on other less important factors. In this case, the best leadership is defined by how the product reaches its consumers, not by the process.self-organizing teamsOne of the most obvious characteristics of an agile environment is that it is made up of self-organizing teams. These are people who know what they are doing. As the project manager, select people who have the skills to meet the project requirements. A self-organizing team works with minimal supervision, believing that the project manager trusts their abilities. Belonging to a stable teamAn agile team is also stable over the long term. With the support and motivation of their project manager, team members will find no reason to leave the company. Therefore, an agile environment consists of stable team members who are ready and willing to support the organization in achieving its goals.face-to-face interactionThis is a reminder of one of the guidelines of an agile project management methodology. In an agile environment, personal interaction is considered the best form of communication. Other forms of communication can be used to ensure that interaction is facilitated regardless of geographic location. However, face-to-face interactions are valued against other forms of com munication.Full transparencyOne of the best things about an agile environment is that no one is left in the dark. Keep in mind that people can quickly access the progress of the project through the task boards. Therefore, if something needs to change, each team member can have a say in what needs to be changed. This transparency in an agile environment creates trust. Team members are more motivated because the organization trusts them enough to share everything about the project.sprintsSprints are at the heart of any agile project management method. It refers to a limited period of time in which the Scrum team works to accomplish a set amount of work. If your organization doesn't work with sprints, you're not working in an agile environment. The best way to gain agility in your organization is to work in sprints. By dividing the project into smaller one-sProjects can easily make necessary changes. Also, one of the main reasons for using sprints is to ensure that the end product reaches the customer. requirements.

Continuous Improvement

Another feature of an agile environment is that it promotes a continuous environment throughout the project development process. When using Agile, the goal is not to deliver a complete product after a certain period of time. Instead, the emphasis is on continually improving a functioning product through the various stages of development. Continuous improvement can identify and resolve product issues. Additionally, the team improves products based on customer needs. With these qualities, you should have an idea of what working in an agile environment should look like. Your organization must embrace the culture where people work together towards a common goal. Working in sprints should also be a no-brainer. Your team should work in short periods of time where they have the opportunity to assess their progress and make adjustments accordingly. More importantly, your business embraces the essence of continuous improvement as a way to meet customer needs. Ultimately, when all of these qualities are present in your business, you can be sure that you are delivering quality products to your customers.For your organization to demonstrate the qualities of an agile environment, you need to address several areas.Transformation to an agile mindset and cultureThe introduction of new technologies has changed the way most businesses work. These technologies have forced people to work in unstable environments where they have to adapt quickly to change. This applies especially to the IT sector, as systems can quickly become obsolete. For organizations to keep up, teams need to be agile. They need to be flexible to adapt to the rapid changes happening around them. It starts with transforming into an agile mindset. How do you create an agile mindset among your team members?Embrace flexibilityA key characteristic of the agile method is that people must be flexible. For example, if a particular strategy is being used to develop a product, team members should have the ability to switch strategies at some point in the development process.Understand the contextAs a project manager, it is crucial for you to understand the complexity of the work environment. If you want to implement an agile method, you must first understand whether the method is applicable or not. In fact, most organizations strive to implement the agile method because it is "in". Since other successful organizations are doing it too, most organizations come to the conclusion that they should be doing it t oo.Of course, the agile method is an ideal technique, but the project manager must be careful when implementing it. They must first understand the complexity of their environment beforehand.Embody the Agile ManifestoFor an organization to develop an agile culture, it must first understand how to live the values of the agile method. These values have been defined in the Agile Manifesto. They differ from the 12 principles discussed at the beginning of this guide. There are four values described in the Agile Manifesto. • People and interactionsThis is the first value of the Agile Manifesto. Here, human interactions are favored over processes and tools. Ideally, these are people who work to meet the needs of each business. They are also the ones who drive the development of an organization. Therefore, they should be held in high regard over processes and tools. In situations where development is done relying heavily on processes and tools, there is a high likelihood that the team is not flexible enough to change. Ultimately, they will not meet consumer needs.• Software via documentationThe idea of documenting every production process took a lot of time back then. This caused delays in the product creation process for software development. The agile method reduces documentation by ensuring that one focuses more on the product than on the process. • Collaboration with customersThe agile method emphasizes the importance of involving the customer in the project development process. Teams should solicit consumer feedback on a regular basis by offering them product demos.• Respond to changeConventional software development teams did their best to avoid change because change was seen as a cost. Changing something during the product development process meant that the team had to start the development process from scratch. The agile method uses sprints to ensure that changes can be easily implemented without having to change the entire product development process. The agile method ensures that a product is constantly improved through change. Added value is added to the product to ensure that customers are satisfied with it.Developing an agile mindset and culture requires team members to remember these values. This manifesto indicates how people should behave in the organization. As a project manager, it's important to coach your team on the importance of knowing these values and sticking to them while working. transparencyTransparency is a fundamental quality that guarantees that the agile method is successfully applied in your organization. Transparency facilitates the development of an agile culture. The people in your organization must rely on a culture of openness to anything that prevents them from achieving the objectives set. The importance of transparency is that it opens doors for review and adjustment. If issues are also identified late in the development process, they can be investigated and resolved before a product is presented to the customer. Everything in the organization should be open, as this encourages a culture of openness. Interestingly, some organizations are transparent about salaries and bonuses. You just need to find a perfect way to impress on your team members the importance of being honest about the project.

Be a Change Agent

Indeed, changing the mentality of people accustomed to a certain way of working is not an easy job. Don't expect change to come overnight. You must be the change agent in your organization. As a project manager, your role is not just to remind your team of their tasks. Rather, it reminds them of agile values. Teach them best practices that lead to an agile environment. This is the best way to develop an agile mindset and culture.Talk to peopleOne big move that can easily destroy your project team's chances of success is to talk about each other. If several teams are working towards a common goal, you shouldn't speak to the management of a particular department's operation. This only diminishes the trust, transparency and respect the team once had. It destroys their morale. It's not for nothing that sprint meetings happen every day. Use this opportunity to talk to them and not about them. If there are issues with the team, identify them during sprint meetings. Remember that to adopt an agile mindset and culture, you need to foster transparency. Creating an Agile mindset and culture starts with ensuring that the project team understands the Agile Manifesto and the importance of embracing the values outlined. Also, as a project manager, you must always remember to set a good example. Change starts with you. You need to lead by showing other team members that you are nimble. You have to prove to them that you are acting without any secrets. Ultimately, people will follow the right path to adopt an agile mindset and culture.How to configure an Agile environmentThe rapidly changing environments we find ourselves in today have transformed industries. Organizations have stepped up their game and understand they need to gain a competitive edge by keeping up with change. For example, organizations gain a competitive advantage over their rivals by leveraging the latest technology. It is the ability to change that makes companies agile and different from others in their industries. An agile organization gives employees the right environment they need to embrace speed and flexibility. To transform into a more agile organization, there are three key areas you need to address.• People• Structure• Process-PeopleThe best place to start transforming your organization to become agile is the human resources department. Conventionally, companies are used to hiring people based on their skills. This leads to a situation where human resources are limited to a certain set of skills. When they hire people, they simply focus on having the specific skills required.To promote agility in your organization, it is imperative to give up a skills checklist. Focus on hiring a team that is not only collaborative but also creative. Find employees curious about new things to entice a customer. Through this approach, an organization creates a flexible and dynamic team. The good news is that a team was put together using this approacheasily adapts to changes that constantly occur during the product development process.structureAn agile work environment can be achieved by removing existing complexities that tend to hamper business processes at all levels. Eliminating these challenges leads to better decisions.The team structure must also be carefully defined. In this case, the role of the project manager is non-traditional. Traditional management strategies assumed that a manager's role was to assign tasks to other employees and ensure that they were carried out appropriately. In an agile work environment, this is not a manager's duty. The role of a manager is to further communicate goals and objectives, key metrics, and motivate the team working on the project. Do you notice the variation?Adopting a traditional hierarchical structure only slows down the way things are done in the organization. Therefore, it is important to adopt the right structure to ensure the creation of a stable and functional agile environment.procedureYou can not only focus on the people and structure of your organization, but also change the processes to create an agile environment. Many companies have processes in place to ensure that a product is developed and delivered to consumers on time. Nevertheless, most of these companies face a major challenge in terms of flexibility. In most cases, they are not flexible enough to quickly adapt to market changes and demands. To work towards an agile environment, organizations must put in place processes that encourage collaboration, rapid decision-making, accountability,Transparency of information, etc. These are some of the attributes that should be evident in an Agile organization.

Chapter Nine

Team Structures

For a For a project to succeed, the project manager must bring together different people with different skills. Your ability to work together towards a common goal determines the success or failure of any project. Many people and different roles can be involved in an agile project team.product ownerAs the name suggests, this is the person with expertise on the product and its requirements. The Product Owner works hand-in-hand with the development team to ensure product requirements are addressed at every stage of development. A product owner could be identified as a customer represen tative.Development team membersIn simple terms, it is the people who create the product. For example, if you are developing software, team members include programmers, designers, testers, data engineers, etc. You should note that members of the development team have different skill sets. This is crucial to achieving the project objectives. Master of meleeThe Scrum Master works closely with the development team. This person works to support the development team by ensuring that the agile process remains consistent throughout the process. Scrum Masters are most effective when they have the power to make changes without necessarily asking for p ermission.StakeholdersStakeholders are individuals who have an interest in the project. They are not responsible for the product. However, they are there to provide the required information. Ultimately, they are affected by project performance. To ensure the success of projects, stakeholders must be involved in the product development process and provide the necessary support at every stage.Agile MentorAn agile method is successfully implemented in an organization by relying on an agile mentor. This is someone who has had direct experience of how the project methodology works. They are there to guide how to apply agility to the organization.Essentially, the idea of creating an Agile workplace comes down to sticking to the Agile Manifesto. For an agile environment to be created in any organization, employees must first understand the core values and principles that they should follow. By following this manifesto, they learn to behave in an agile way.

Chapter Ten

Tools for Quality Control in Agile Project Management

Managing Projects are not an easy task. For this reason, there are several agile tools to help meet the management challenge. A fundamental step in any management process is to ensure that product quality requirements are met. In order to ensure that the agile method is successfully implemented, it is therefore essential to use quality control tools. There are several quality control tools that can be used and some are covered in this chapter. Meeting quality requirements during the development of a product is always an important constraint of the project. In order to ensure that the quality of a product meets requirements, three quality management processes should be followed, which include planning, performing quality assurance, and quality control. Depending on the process, different tools are used. However, some tools can be used interchangeably.A closer examination of the 12 principles of agile project management shows that they directly or indirectly promote the development of a quality product. Before going into the details of quality control tools, consider the notable difference between quality management in traditional approaches and those in agile methods.First, in traditional approaches, product testing was addressed in the final stage of the project development process. Most of the features have been tested months or years after creation. Every day is tested in agile. When running daily sprints, tests are run to ensure thisthe requirements are met. Automated product testing is done to ensure the process is fast and efficient.Even if problems are identified in the later stages of product development, it poses a huge risk to the process. Using the agile method ensures that errors are identified early enough and do not endanger the development process.Given the need to meet project deadlines, traditional approaches often shorten the testing phase. As a result, this leads to the placing on the market of defective products. The Agile method performs regular testing to ensure product quality requirements are met.Product defects, in particular, are costly when discovered in the late stages of development. This applies to traditional quality management approaches. On the other hand, since problems can be easily identified at any stage of the Agile development process, these problems are not expensive to solve.When choosing the right agile tools, it is important to have criteria that help make the right choice. For this reason, there are several tools. Choosing just one is not the best way to find the best quality control tool. Features to consider are task management, integrations, team collaboration, agile metrics, and reporting and analytics.To cleanWhen working on specific projects, there are undeniably activities or processes that are repeatable. The idea of going through all these activities at every stage of product development is a waste of time. An automation tool is useful in this case. Clarizen serves the purpose because it is an automationsoftware solutions. A company with several related activities can use this software to transform its business operations. Service automation will speed up processes and lead to efficiency.Clarizen helps with to-do list, calendars, notifications, documents and files, and reports. During the project execution phase, the software ensures that all team members are on the same page. Each project employee can find out how their contribution helps the team.Tre lloAnother highly recommended agile tool is Trello. If you are new to the world of agile project management, this tool is for you. Trello is considered one of the simplest project management tools available. The best thing about this tool is that you can see it in action without paying a dime. With its simplicity, there are specific features that are not available in the free version of the tool. However, for the best functionality, you have to pay for the full version.GitScrumGitScrum is a project management tool that will help any project manager use agile. This tool stands out from the others by some unique features it offers. For example, it has a time tracking tool that helps to log hours. In addition, it has a bug tracking feature, which allows the user to get bug reports and check their status. Useful Scrum features in the product include a project calendar, checklists, change log, customizable workflows, sprint planning, and reporting tools such as burndown charts. This tool allows the project team to upload andshare files and communicate through discussion forums, as well as stay up to date via email notifications.JiraWhen looking for the best agile project management tools, you will likely find Jira because it is widely used. Initially, Jira was used to review bugs and track issues. However, over time it has evolved into a mature and agile tool. With this tool, task management, reporting, and team collaboration become relatively easy.One of the main benefits of using Jira is that it provides flexibility in managing unique workflows. This allows the user to customize the workflow and process to suit their project. It also offers the advantage of integrations. Users can take advantage of the seven-day trial period to see if Jira works for them.taigaTaiga is a simple and easy to use open source project management tool. More importantly, it is powerful. Its functionality is focused on Kanban and Scrum and it can easily create backlogs with Sprints, User Stories and Epics. Taiga allows for social management, which helps teams when they need to help each other. In addition, there are other components for team collaboration and task management for users.

However, the weakness is in the integration and reporting aspects .

Pivotal

Tracker

Project development, which follows the Kanban style, is best managed with Pivotal Tracker. This tool is suitable for task management. Well-organized workspaces make it easy to manage multiple projects. The workspaces are also arranged in such a way that a user can easily identify their priorities. There are also great analytical tools that help you better understand the health of the project. Reporting using this tool provides a quick snapshot of project performance. In addition to these great features, the tool also takes integrations seriously. Therefore, you will find useful integrations like Slack, Zendeck, and GitHub. Smaller teams of less than three people can use this tool for free. However, larger teams will have to pay for the features offered by Pivotal Tracker. boatswainPeople working on digital projects will benefit from the Nostromo all-in-one. Ideal features including time management, task management, reporting, analytics and to-do lists. Being a new project management tool on the market, few integrations are available.HansHanssoft is the ideal choice for many due to its adaptability. Organizations that tend to scale quickly should use this agile project management tool. The package also includes a number of learning tools, including courses and webinars.Hansof exceeds expectations when it comes to managing arrears. Users can easily group items based on themes, sprints and epics. Items can also be prioritized before being assigned to a particular sprint. The priority view of items helps users work effectively on the most pressing issues first. Likewise, there are intuitive dashboards to provide all team members with the information they need during the project development process. This confirms that better and better decisions are being made regarding the project.FlowerDistributed teams can take advantage of Blossom's project management tool. The customizable workflow shows the status of the project. Blossom makes it easy to add comments, files, to-do lists, and more. The easy to use interface is simple and allows the team to see activity on the project.Similarly, there are performance analysis tools that help measure the performance of a project from its conception to the delivery of the final product. Blossom is also good with integrations .ravenRavetree is another good project management tool. Unlike other tools, Ravetree is not limited to use by software teams. Any agile organization can take advantage of the unique features that include resource planning, time tracking, expense tracking, CRM, and digital asset management. Ravetree has a very intuitive interface that makes it easy for team members to find the information they need.This list is just a summary of some of the best agile project management tools. There are various features that distinguish these tools. Therefore, it is important that you go through its features and determine if it is the best agile tool for you. The trial periodit can be a great way to test the product without paying for it. Don't forget the importance of probationary periods provided.

Chapter Eleven

Managing Risk in Agile Project Management

When When working on projects, managers and product owners often understand that there are risks involved in working on the project. Anything can happen when developing a product to bring to market. Customers could either accept or reject the products, or the released product could pass or f ail.The notion of risk taking implies that there are possibilities of failure in the process. This is why we talk about risk taking. Otherwise it would have been called a safety grip. Risks are therefore influential factors that damage the outcome of a project. The risk arises from uncertainty. Project managers do their best to deliver a quality product despite the many uncertainties they face. Risk analysis allows a team working on a project to understand the likely uncertainties they may face. Risk management is the plan that the team formulates to mitigate the effects that can pose a risk to the success of a project. When managing projects, things can easily go wrong. It doesn't matter if you are working on a small or large project; sometimes things go wrong. It is essential to ensure that there is a plan in place to minimize the potential impact when unpredictable events occur. What follows is a look at how risk management should be performed in an agile environment. Step 1: IdentifyThe first step is to identify the dimensions of risk. There are two aspects where risks could be taken. It can be either helpful or harmful, either internal or external. There could be a SWOT analysis that could help understand how the risks affect the project. For example, if the risk is useful, it can be seen as a strength or an opportunity. On the other hand, if the risk is harmful, it can be a major weakness or a threat.The idea of risk management mainly focuses on what is harmful. In this case, some of the main weaknesses that a project might suffer from include insufficient resources, aggressive schedule, limited budget, technological uncertainties, lack of essential skills in the team, etc. Threats one could face include pandemics, economic uncertainty, trade tariffs, changing laws, and geopolitical tensions. A closer look at threats and weaknesses reveals that weaknesses are things that can be controlled while threats are things that cannot be easily controlled. While people may not have control over things like disease, there are measures that can be taken to reduce the effects of risk on projects.Step 2: rankOnce the risks have been identified, the next step is to classify them. The classification should be based on the affected areas. Grouping should be done based on the likelihood of risk. Likewise, the degree of impact will also be an important consideration in the classification of identified risks. Step 3: QuantizeOnce the risks have been classified according to their extent, their probability of occurrence or the areas affected, the next step is quantification.She. This is where you measure the impact of the risk, or the likely impact of the risk if it occurs. Certainly, a risk assessment must be carried out by an expert. For example, when security systems are being evaluated, this is something the project manager cannot handle unless qualified in the field. The same goes for other aspects that need to be evaluated, including quality, performance, and privacy. Keeping in mind that an agile environment promotes transparency, the team should sit down together and discuss the results of the assessment. This will go a long way in bringing friendly solutions to the table.Risks can be quantified based on impact and probability. The impact of risk measures the effect it has on a project. Here the impact can range from minimal to extreme. Minimal impact means there is little impact a particular risk could have on the project.However, this does not mean that the risk should be ignored. Conversely, the risk should be assessed on a regular basis to confirm that it has been adequately mitigated. The impact classified as extreme means that it can lead to the failure of a project. The extreme impact also damages the budget and timing of the project. In the worst cases, these risks can put the entire organization at risk.With respect to probability, the occurrence of risk can be quantified from very unlikely to very likely. If the risk can occur easily, it can be classified as probable or very probable. Conversely, if there is little chance of it happening, then it can be classified as unlikely or very unlikely occur.

Step

4:

Plan

To at this point you have identified and classified the potential risks that may arise during the management of a project in the organization. So what should be done about these risks? Risk planning comes into play. You have to find a simple approach to address these risks. The plan should identify the actions that will be used to effectively manage risks. For example, when dealing with risks that have minimal impact on the project, it would be ideal to review the risks on a quarterly basis. It should also be clarified that no explicit action is required because the risks do not constitute harm.On the other hand, critical risks require urgent attention. Your plan should also specifically state that a responsible manager should be notified. A critical risk must be monitored daily to ensure that its impact is significantly reduced. Depending on how the risks are classified, your plan should clearly state what action to take. In an agile environment, the risk plan should be accessible to all members working on a project. This helps ensure that the team knows what actions to take depending on the risk taken.To ensure that risks are continuously managed, it is important to have a risk register. This is a register in which risks and related mitigation strategies are recorded. The importance of this register is that it shows how a particular risk has changed since it was identified. If the risk was critical, the management strategies used should ensure that the risk falls into the minimum category. This gives everyone the assurance that the risks have been managed effectively.Step 5: ActThe final step in risk management is to take action. Essentially, you are implementing what has been specified in the risk mitigation strategies. However, the process isn't as simple as it sounds. People are often used to putting things off for a later date. This makes risk management unnecessary. Risks need to be addressed as soon as they are identified. Remember that working in an agile environment means acting fast. Step 6: RepeatThe risk management process in an agile environment means you have to repeat the process over and over again. It is a vicious circle to guarantee the success of your project. It is important to note that the risk plan used should be reviewed regularly to ensure that optimal mitigation measures are applied to potential risks.Risk management will always be part of any project. Considering that many uncertainties can arise, it is imperative to put in place a risk management strategy. The steps outlined here are designed to help you create a practical risk management plan. Note that a risk management strategy that works for another organization may not necessarily work for you. Different companies face different risks whether or not they develop similar products not.

Chapter Twelve

The Main Benefits of Applying the Agile Method

At the At the beginning of this guide, we discussed several benefits of using the agile project management method. This section takes a closer look at the key benefits organizations gain when they choose to use the agile method. In other words, we'll explore some of the main reasons why the agile method is so compelling.Quick identification of wrong approachesObviously, in a more traditional project management method, when the wrong path is used, it probably means that the entire project development process is compromised. In extreme cases, the entire project development process should be abandoned. This can cost the organization a lot of money because a product cannot be marketed unless it meets consumer demands.The use of the agile method supports the fail-fast strategy. This is an approach where product developers try to get quick feedback from customers or end users. Upon receiving a response, changes are made quickly to ensure that the product meets customer requirements in every way.Since there are many uncertainties to be addressed, it is cheaper to get a product to market quickly and find out if it works or not. If the product is not functional, it can be discontinued immediately without additional money, hence the term "fail-fast". With the agile concept, incorrect procedures can be quickly identified. Ultimately, a company will save a lot of time and money that would have been wasted trying to launch a product that doesn't meet market demand.Quick decision makingAn agile environment brings together individuals in an organization to recognize that their combined efforts are helping to achieve project goals. Quick decisions can be made in daily meetings. Team members are fully aware that the agile method requires personal interactions to be valued. Cooperation offers many advantagesThe idea of working in a collaborative environment has benefits for the entire organization. In this case, people working towards a common goal also share a common desire to succeed. People and technology resources can work together to quickly achieve project goals. In a rapidly changing environment, the use of agile tools comes in handy. These tools help ensure that things are done efficiently. For example, if repetitive processes are present, agile tools conveniently confirm that those processes are automated. On the other hand, people work together to solve new and existing problems that can hinder the success of any project.There are many benefits of the project through collaboration.1. The need for frequent changes due to poorly understood requirements is greatly reduced. Because team members work transparently, they can clearly define product requirements. Therefore, it reduces the need to come and go when these requirements are not fully met.2. Collaboration also helps a lot in identifying risks. Risks are identified quickly and therefore dealt with effectively. 3. A team that works in harmony can easily realize their true potential because they can identify their strengths and weaknesses. The team can work to exploit these strengths while doing their best to address their weaknesses.4. Collaboration also ensures that continuous improvement is maintained throughout the product development process. 5. If cooperation within the organization improves, this also has a positive effect on the organization. You can easily adapt to sudden changes. In other words, the organization becomes more agile when working with a collaborative team team.

Chapter Thirteen

Change is Embraced

Working in an agile environment also fosters the quick adaptability to change. During the product development process, the importance of adapting quickly to change is a fact that the agile method promotes. Ideally, the push for change is one of the core values of the agile method. Therefore, as teams learn to make changes more often, they develop a culture where change is embraced regardless of the development stage. In this case, people understand that change leads to an improved product being delivered to consumers.

Chapter Fourteen

A Final Product with Useful Features

The the best thing about using the agile method is that the product is constantly evolving. Usually, a demo product is introduced to the market to get feedback from consumers, so customers contribute a lot to the development process. When the product is finally launched, it will have all the features a customer could want. The chances of the product being successful in the market are high because it has all the features a customer desires. Getting the market's attention isn't a challenge. An environment suitable for millennialsMillennials are the next generation to take over the many jobs of baby boomers.

The good news is that the fast-paced environment is exactly what millennials love. Workplace agility will therefore benefit millennials who work in multiple organizations. As a result, creating an agile environment ensures that employees feel motivated to work towards achieving business goals.Deliver the right productAbove all, a major advantage of the agile method is that the right product is delivered to consumers. Since a product is carefully checked daily during each sprint meeting, any defects can be identified at an early stage. In addition, regular checks ensure that product requirements are met. If something goes wrong, it can be quickly changed at any stage of the development process. The end product is almost perfect because the customer gets a product that has all the expected properties.An exciting work environmentAn agile environment is an environment that encourages active participation, collaboration, and collaboration among team members. This is an experience that excites many when they can share tasks. Through this collaboration, the team also helps each other overcome their weaknesses. So it is not only the organization that benefits from the agile method, but also the employees who use it. This ensures that employees are motivated every time they work on a project. There is no denying that such a positive attitude on the part of employees translates into greater productivity at work. Focus on business valueOne of the most important core values of the agile method is that it values people and interactions over processes and tools. Therefore, the agile method guarantees closer involvement of stakeholders in the development process. This helps ensure that the team understands the organization's mission and vision. The team will focus more on the most important tasks during the product development process. They highly value their cooperation and collaboration, which results in bringing a high-quality product to market at the right time and within budget. transparencyThe agile method is synonymous with transparency. Everything related to the project is always discussed openly with interested parties and the development team. Since customers are also involved in the process, it helps to prioritize features and fix bugs. Nevertheless, it is important that developers inform customers that they are using demo products and not real products. Clean air avoids confusion and leads to reliable customer feedback data. Tailor-made team structuresThe concept of self-management creates a work environment in which teams can make decisions independently. An agile workplace creates opportunities for employees to customize their work tasks. This means that they can choose to work according to the rules that suit them. The adjustment of team structures can go in any direction. A group can be organized according to working styles. Another team could be organized according to their respective capacities. Such an adjustment creates a friendly workplace where employees are highly motivated.Improved project predictabilityUsing the agile project management method also helps a team predict the progress of the project. Improved predictability can be achieved by ensuring sprint lengths are always the same. In addition, the distribution of tasks should not be changed during the entire development process. With these practices, it is easy to predict the progress or outcome of a project.Improved team moralePeople who love what they do are motivated to work without being pushed around. Working in an autonomous team paves the way for creativity and innovation. What is exciting is that the respective groups will focus on sustainability. Therefore, team members are not stressed by work-related issues. Remember that a supportive environment also positively affects the way people work.There are many reasons why the agile method is so great. Using the agile project management method increases the chances of a product's success on the market. Likewise, with the collaborative environment in which team members work, they adopt a culture where the need for change drives them. All in all, this benefits the organization in both the short and long term. So, are you still hesitating to use the agile project management method? Considering the advantages mentioned, you can be sure that there is even more to be gained by using this method of project management..

Chapter Fifteen

Common Challenges in Using the Agile Method

Considering the advantages of the agile method, it is surprising that most organizations do not use it. Most organizations that use it don't have the expected success either. Using the agile project management method does not guarantee that a project will automatically succeed. Those who implement the agile method face common challenges. This chapter discusses these challenges and offers solutions. Knowing these challenges helps you understand the factors that stand in the way of success. Users can adjust accordingly by avoiding regular pitfalls.I refuse to accept the changeOne of the biggest challenges for organizations looking to implement the agile method of project management is their reluctance to accept change. People have a hard time changing the cultures they are used to. Project managers find it a huge challenge to apply an agile framework. To ensure that the agile method is applied successfully, it is vital that the organization understands the importance of embracing new ideas. It is essential to note that once senior executives recognize the value of change, they will set an example to strive for a successful implementation of the agile methodology.Distributed teamImplementing the agile method also becomes a challenge when the team working on a project is not in the same place. The success of theproject is affected by geographical boundaries. People with different time zones sometimes have a hard time working together. Collaboration is therefore difficult to achieve. Ineffective communication influenced by missing team members will lead to a drop in produ ctivity.Change team membershipThe progress made initially may all vanish as team membership continues to change. In reality, the team needs time to make up for lost time when team members change. If this continues to happen, it means the team is unstable. This also affects team morale as they feel wasted when they have to repeat activities. For a team to gain stability, it is essential that the project manager put together a team that will work together for the long term. Of course, some circumstances could force team members to leave. However, such events should be reduced by keeping people motiva ted.Self-organizationBut when it comes to changing team membership, this poses a huge challenge for self-organization. It is discouraging for team members to complete tasks alone when employees leave the team. Moreover, self-organization is not easy to achieve anyway. It does not automatically result from the composition of a group of qualified people. A project manager should regularly coach the team and constantly remind them of agile principles and core values. All of this takes time, which is a major challenge for most businesses. Lack of qualified Product OwnersThe agile project management method is new to most business analysts and stakeholders. It is therefore difficult for them to give up their traditional way of working. Some of them believe, to some extent, that the transparency encouraged by Agile prevents them from having complete control of things. What they forget is that the agile method does not require stakeholders to constantly push people around. Instead, self-organizing teams ensure tasks are completed with minimal supervision. The absence of qualified product owners therefore makes the full application of the agile method a challenge.Tactical problemsUsing the agile project management method requires that users be provided with the necessary tools for quality and risk management. These tools help promote work efficiency. If these tools are not provided by the organization, it is difficult to achieve the level of agility that the organization expects.Not familiar with the techniquesThe adoption of the agile method means that the different departments must be trained on how to implement the strategies in their routine activities and on how to use these tools. The process can be time-consuming, which often discourages organizations from adopting the management method in the first place.Realize these challenges, realize that agile is not as simple as it seems. It's a process that looks simple on paper. However, the implementation process is something entirely different. This is where most people fail. Teams working on a project can't just read a book and adopt an agile culture. Itit does not work like this. It takes a long time to create an agile environment and cultivate an agile culture in the organization. Keep in mind that you are pushing for change in an organization that has taken a traditional approach for decades. That's why you need to be patient and focused when implementing agile method.

Chapter Sixteen

How Agile Can Easily Fail

It is also crucial for you to learn a thing or two about how you can fail when using the agile approach. There is no agile technique where the goal is failure. However, poor planning by an informed team can easily lead to defeat. You might be using the best agile method, but it won't work if you don't use the right approach. The following lines explain how things can go wrong with an agile strategy. This information gives you the information you need to avoid common pitfalls that could prevent your business from succeeding.Plan chaoticallyA common myth surrounding the use of Agile is that planning is not important. It's not true. Even if an agile system is in place, that doesn't mean planning isn't important. Planning is the best way to execute your strategy. Luckily, there's a tool your team can use to effectively plan and align their actions with business goals. This tool is called Agile Release Train and it can help a company plan projects even twelve months in advance.Form an unstable teamWe talked a lot about collaboration. The success of any agile program depends on your team's ability to combine their efforts. When you work with a team of people who get along well, you have thisthe top. Conversely, if your team is made up of strangers, it will discourage you from achieving the success you want to achieve.Teams need to be optimized to reduce dependencies. An ideal group should be made up of individuals who understand the specifics of their work. They shouldn't wait for the project manager to guide them constantly. The best agile teams are made up of generalists. These are experts who do not depend on other groups of specialists to carry out their tasks.Rarely communicateAgile teams with poor communication will fail quickly. The flow of communication in an agile environment must be continuous. A regular exchange must be maintained with stakeholders interested in the final product. The project manager must ensure that everyone in the organization speaks on similar wavelengths. It is very likely that some terminology will be used in the workplace. A good team should have a unified vocabulary about the product.Poor product testsRegular testing ensures that quality is maintained in product development. The bad test is the fast track to failure. It is critical for developers to rigorously test products to make sure they meet standards. Regular testing helps the team easily adapt to changes.Not understanding the scope of the projectFor the agile management approach to work optimally, it is crucial that the project manager creates a roadmap. This roadmap guides the development team on how to accomplish the tasks. It defines the path to follow to ensure that a working product is obtained at the end of each sprint. Therefore, it is important that all team members understand the scope of the project from the start. This ensures that each step is aligned with the objectives of the project.Ignore customer feedbackCustomer feedback is what will bring about changes in the agile system. Not listening to the consumer's evaluation only leads to frustration. Your team will be disappointed that they didn't succeed despite their best efforts. Customer feedback should be a top priority as it ensures full compliance with product requirements. The lack of customer feed-back makes knowing how to prioritize a daunting task. In the end, the development team might over-look what's most important to them. the customer.

Chapter Seventeen

Tips and Tricks to Make Your Agile Project Management System Efficient

Undeniably, several teams were able to use the agile project management method and achieve variable results. Some will succeed in using the agile method while others may fail. The point here is that how the agile method is implemented makes a huge difference in the success or failure of a project. This chapter discusses some tips that can help ensure the efficiency of the agile project management s ystem.Use of time management techniquesOne of the most important things to consider when working with an agile team is time management. As a project manager, it is imperative that people manage their time effectively as they would perform a wide variety of activities in the organization. Therefore, it is essential that the project manager carries out all these activities at the same time ensuring fast delivery times.To help you plan your day, use agile tools to help you keep track of what needs to be done. Agile tools easily schedule ongoing tasks for you and your team to complete.In situations where you are not tech-savvy, you can use a simple to-do list. This list will serve as a reminder of what needs to be done at any given time. Confirm that important tasks take precedence over others. As a project manager, making the most of your time ensures that planned activities are not delayed. Ultimately, projects will be completed in a timely manner without skipping requirements.Indicate the requirements of the projectThe success of a project is determined by the result. This means that when the project is completed, the end product is what decides whether the project was a success or not. Accordingly, the success of the project is measured by whether the product meets all the requirements expected by consumers. Therefore, for a project to be successful, it is necessary to outline the requirements of the project. This is a fundamental step that ensures the development team understands what needs to be done. The project manager must coordinate the tasks leading to the realization of the project requirements. Ideally, this is the most important.Hire a qualified project managerThe agile project management system will not work optimally without a qualified project manager. This person with sufficient experience will understand what needs to be done for a particular project to be successful. Likewise, a credible manager knows how to assign tasks to different people based on their qualifications. More importantly, they will find a way to ensure that the process is not only productive but exciting at the same time. When things go wrong in the project development process, an ideal manager steps in and proposes friendly solutions. Most importantly, they also know how to gain customer trust through effective communication. Therefore, a skilled project manager gets the information he needs from trusted customers about what needs to be changed in a product to meet consumer needs. In fact, there are many reasons why hiring the right manager should:given priority, as they are the general drivers of the project: choosing the wrong person for the task will only risk the failure of the project.Offer regular updates and demos-The best way to keep an agile project efficient is to communicate the progress of the project on a regular basis. This means that both interested parties and customers must be kept informed of the progress of the product. Also, a project manager must communicate with them about their tasks. They should be aware that their contribution helps make the project a success.When the project is underway, they need to be constantly updated on product features and deadlines. If there is a problem with the product, this information should reach them as well. Effective communication confirms that the project is progressing smoothly and with minimal disruptio n.Additionally, stakeholders and customers should benefit from demonstrations while the product is still “in the kitchen”. Don't wait until your cake is fully baked to present it to them. It could be risky for your organization if changes were to be made. Therefore, it is wise to offer demos to gauge consumer reaction to the product even before it hits the market. Remember the "fail fast" aspect? It will save you a lot of money if the product is not what consumers want. Plus, quick changes can be made to the product without impacting your business p erformance.Regular communication with your tea- mEnsuring your team communicates regularly has many benefits. It is undeniable that more frequent communication avoids misunderstandings. If there are unclear requirements that the team does not understand, these can also be ironed out through regular communication. Making sure your team is informed about every step they take increases the chances of project success. Define critical milestonesThe success of a project largely depends on the main stages to which particular attention should be paid. As a project manager, you must ensure that these phases are identified as the project progresses. Team members should understand that some phases are more important than others. To ensure that the phases are successful, it is important that the project manager conducts an evaluation after the end of each phase. Before proceeding to the next phase, the project manager should confirm that the project requirements have been fully met. In the end, when all the steps come together, there is a high probability that the project will succeed. Defining critical milestones serves as an indicator that the team is doing its best to complete the project's goals.

Anticipating

Project

Setbacks

In spite With your well-thought-out plan, you should always expect something to go wrong. It doesn't matter if you've hired the best project manager in town or not. Anything can happen to your project. How you handle the challenges you face will have a major impact on the overall performance of the project. For safety, pay attention to the warning signs. Check for missed deadlines, listen to stakeholder complaints and any other signs that may indicate problems with theproject. Addressing these issues will get you back on track and deliver a quality product on time.Keep in mind that preventing a crisis will keep your project on track. Plus, your team can be confident that the project will go as planned. So it is essential for any project manager to anticipate setbacks and learn how to manage them effectively. Unfortunately, not all challenges or crises can be solved. There are some obstacles that could burn the whole project. However, crisis management skills come in handy in these cases. Project managers must learn to deal with situations they least expect. They need to be flexible to change and confident that they can make quick decisions when working in an agile environment. project evaluationAnother tip that will ensure your agile project thrives is evaluation. Any project you work on should be considered a learning tool. A good manager takes the time to review project performance. All components of the project should be evaluated to see if certain areas could be improved in future projects. By learning from past performance, a project manager can find ideal opportunities for improvement in the future. transition supportIBenefits that can be obtained by adopting the agile method. Coaching should be there to support mistakes. Really, don't expect your team to be perfect as soon as you adopt Agile. Give them time to adjust.Support should also be provided in the form of mentoring in specific roles. Some team members may pick up the method faster than others. That doesn't mean you have to leave others behind. As a project manager, you work to empower each person and ensure they are aligned with the other members. This brings stability to your development team. Ultimately, you increase the likelihood of a successful project. Total openness and transparencyOnce you have implemented the agile method in your organization, there is nothing left to hide. You can't hide the way people do things. You cannot hide project progress. The poor quality of your product cannot be hidden because you are going to test it with consumers. Nothing is hidden in an agile environment. Here's what your optimal agile environment should look like. The agile tools you use should help you maximize the quality of the output. Full openness and transparency ensure the resolution of existing challenges, which are clearly visible in the project development process. That's why it all starts with setting the perfect example, being open and transparent in how you interact with your team.Early feedbackdevelops, consumers should test the demo product. They need to know how it works. This way, the team receives timely feedback and can make changes where necessary. Getting timely feedback allows the team to easily adapt to changes. Most importantly, early feedback also helps ensure that the right product is delivered to the customer. It reduces the risk of speculation. Knowing what the client wants and striving to meet their needs increases the chances of project success.value on activityThe idea of working in an agile environment can be confusing to many. Yes, agility requires rapid changes to be made to every process. However, to be successful in your agile system, your team must prioritize value over activity. Your goal shouldn't just be to get things done. On the contrary, the focus should be more on value creation. To ensure this point is internalized, your team should revisit the core values outlined in the Agile Manifesto.Shared responsibilityYour agile system will thrive when you develop a culture where no one is held accountable for their part. The team working on a project must appreciate the importance of shared responsibility. All team members should be responsible for the outcome of the project. This means that if something goes wrong, the whole team is to blame. In this way, individuals understand the importance of working together for a common goal. Collaboration leads to greater productivity. So this is what the project manager should support.A closer look at tips and tricks reveals the values and principles promoted by the Agile Manifesto. For any agile system to be successful in the long run, people and interactions must be weighed against processes or tools. It is the way people interact with each other that contributes to the success of a project. Project developers are the people who respond to the consumer's wishes; so this is a value that should be kept.Likewise, consumers should be involved in the product development process. This helps ensure that their expectations are met and met by providing them with product demos at every stage of the development process. This gives the development team insight into what needs to be done to ensure that a product meets customer req uirements.Remember that agility is also more about being responsive to change. The advent of the Internet has changed the way businesses behave in their respective industries. Today, these companies find themselves in a volatile environment and to keep pace, they must embrace change. Without transition, customers will shift to competing products as they meet their ever-changing needs. For an agile system to work successfully, it must change inevitable.

Chapter Eighteen

Key Metrics to Measure Agile Success

So, after you successfully implement your agile method, you want to know if it was successful or not. How do you know if the agile system has made a difference? Chances are you are thinking about product quality, as the agile method promotes the idea of focusing on the product and not the process. Well, you need to understand that there is more to being successful in agile than just providing a quality product. This chapter will help you understand the key metrics to help you measure the success level of your agile system. Before measuring Agile success, you need to ask yourself a few questions.• Does the organization have an agile culture?The success of your organization is determined by its agile maturity. All departments in your organization must have reached a certain level of maturity since the development of the agile system. The way processes are managed also says a lot about how the agile culture has transformed your team. For example, if you see sprint meetings happening daily, that means your team has changed. Since you know the agile values, your team's actions must be aligned with these values.• Is the organization credible?Additionally, you need to focus on whether your team is delivering the promised product to the customer. This is a simple process as you only need to confirm that the end product requirements have been met. An agile system that helps the team meet customer requirements can be identified as a good system. WithOver time, your business will earn the credibility it seeks by producing the highest quality products.• Does the organization respect its commitments?It is also crucial for the project manager to check whether the organization is meeting its commitments through the application of the agile technique. Its obligations relate here to the properties of the product and the respect of the deadlines of the project. Likewise, the company must deliver the product on time as promised to the customers. The speed of a team will have a major impact on the respect of the group's commitments. The secret effort of the whole team is to complete a series of tasks within a given time frame.• Does the organization produce quality products?The answer to this question illustrates the performance of the company. If the team produces quality products, it means they perform well. Conversely, defective products mean that something is wrong with the agile system used.The following are essential metrics that will help you measure the success of your agile system.Timely deliveryAn important metric by which you can measure the success of your agile initiative is on-time product delivery.

By meeting customer expectations, you can measure the degree of success. A product that arrives on the market at the right time gains a competitive advantage over its competitors in the market. People will want to use the products that hit the market first.If the product meets their requirements, there's a good chance they'll stick with that product in the long run. Measuring the success of an agile initiative through timely delivery is done through burn-up charts. These are tools that help project managers keep track of the progress of a project. These charts provide the development team with the information they need to plan completion dates. The charts also help them ensure that the process is on schedule.p roduct qualityThe quality of the product also says a lot about the agile method. The quality of the product influences the success of the project in several ways. First, it will have a big impact on customer satisfaction. A product that satisfies customer needs performs well in the market. This means that the project has been completed. Moreover, a project is successful because the income from the sale of the product meets the objectives of the organization. The quality of the products speaks volumes about the performance of the company in many ways.cli ent satisfactionThe success of your agile system can also be measured by customer satisfaction. Here you have to consider the sales figures. If the product sells in the market, it is a clear sign that you have done well. Your efforts to deliver a good product will pay off. You can also consider the number of calls you receive regarding the product. If many calls ask for details, it means your project went well. Simply put, customers will be happy with what you delivered and therefore your return on investment. high.

Business

Value

The The overall business value gained from using the agile method is also used to measure how good your agile system is. It is important to remember that this is what the Agile Manifesto promotes. Corporate value is highly valued above all else. Business value is achieved when contract requirements are met or when a product is delivered at the right time.Produ ct scope:You can also measure the success of your agile initiative by looking at the size of the product. At the beginning of the development process, set goals related to the features and requirements you need to have for a particular product. At the end of the process, it is really worth achieving these goals. As such, knowing that the product delivered to market meets all the requirements the product owner expects is a sign that the project is a success. It is a clear indication that the agile method has worked.Visibility of the projectThe level of success of your agile method can also be determined by its visibility. The best agile system is one in which everything is open to the whole team. Knowing that all members interested in the project are aware of its progress is one way to determine its success. It would not have been successful if the cases had not been made public.Process improvementIt is also possible to measure the performance of your agile system through process improvement. One of the main reasons why the agile method leads to an overall improvement in product quality is the idea of continuous improvement. The frequent changes after each sprint ultimately determine the quality of the product. If the product is continuously improved at every stage, it means that the final product will be what the customer expects. Thus, your agile method should improve things throughout the project development process.satisfaction surveysThe highest priority of any Agile program is meeting customer needs. One way to know if this objective is achieved is to carry out satisfaction surveys. Customers can use the demo products and help to know if their requirements are met. Satisfaction surveys can also be completed by team members. In this case, members answer questions about their experience of working with the organization. Such group studies identify the loopholes that exist in the product development group.crackingDefects will always be part of any project. No matter how experienced the development team is, there will be errors in the product development process. Any good team should work to ensure that mistakes are kept to a minimum. The idea of debugging also helps to measure the performance of the agile program. The team working on a new product knows how well it does it to avoid glitches in the development process.Project managers want to know how their agile initiatives are doing. Therefore, it is imperative for them to consider the metrics mentioned in this section. It would be difficult to determine which direction you are going without knowing whether or not you are succeeding in the first place. Project managers need to look at the quality of their product. Do they provide the best quality product on the market? If so, will this product reach the consumer at the right time? Additionally, they should also look at customer satisfaction. Are customers satisfied with the product? These metrics give project managers a deeper insight into their level of performance. More importantly, they must try to continuously improve as this is the best way to counter the competition in the industry. market.

Chapter Nineteen

Final Thoughts

Congratulations to get to this part of the book. By now you understand what agile project management is. Of course, when managing projects, every manager wants to make sure their project is successful. Unfortunately, most of them use a traditional approach to project management. This makes it difficult to market a product that matches the customer's wishes. The agile method of project management is a new way of approaching projects by promoting rapid changes in the project development process. The agile method was introduced after software developers struggled to deliver their products on time using the traditional approach. Using this technique, they turned in applications late and sometimes their projects were canceled. This happened due to the delays that affected the delivery of the products on schedule.After the frustrations of software developers, they had to come up with a method that is more about the product and not the process. They wanted to make sure a product reached the consumer as quickly as possible. Fast delivery of software products was the only way developers could understand what customers wanted and make the necessary changes. This led to Agile Project Management. Sure, the method was introduced for the benefit of software developers, but it can also be used in any organization. The idea of managing projects occurs in every institution. Therefore, using the agile method can be an effective way to guarantee the success of a projec t.As a reminder, the agile method has 12 principles that determine how a project should be managed. The highest priority of an Agile project is to meet customer requirements through rapid and continuous delivery. Likewise,change must be recognized at all stages of the development process. The agile method also promotes the idea that the project is built around a group of motivated people. Therefore, no one needs to be rushed to achieve their daily goals.When using the agile method, personal conversation is considered the most effective form of communication. Technology has changed the way people communicate. There are social platforms that facilitate interaction between people, regardless of their geographical location. Nevertheless, when applying the agile method, the personal exchange is very much appreciated. This is the best way to get quick feedback on the progress of the project. Furthermore, an agile environment revolves around simplicity. The project manager should strive to reduce any complexity in the development process. They should define each path so that it is easy for the team to focus more on delivering a product that meets customer requirements. Do not forget; there are regular inspections at every stage of the product development process. This guarantees the effectiveness of a product in the eyes of the con sumer.But it should be noted that the process of implementing the agile project management method is not as simple as it seems. A project manager must be careful not to implement the method until he understands certain aspects of the organization, including their willingness to take risks, team agility and their risk aversion. Knowing this sets the right platform to implement a method that will work with the organization. There is no doubt that it would not be practical to use this strategy in an environment where the team is not agile. So it is important to consider the aspects of the organization before taking any action.Implementing the agile method not only requires the organization to create an agile environment, but also to transform its mindset. You can't have an agile environment if employees don't have an agile mindset. In this case, the individuals in the organization must believe in the need for change. Likewise, they need to be flexible enough to adapt to rapid changes. To transform people's mindsets, they also need to understand what the Agile Manifesto promotes. They need to be well informed about the four core values and principles of the manifesto.Likewise, your organization needs an agile environment that supports an agile way of working. How can this be achieved? From the lessons learned, focus on the people, the structure and the process. Creating an agile environment starts with recruiting the right people to work on the project. HR needs to understand that when hiring employees, they need to focus on the big picture. In addition to their skills, they must also take into account their creativity and their ability to work in a team. Individuals should also be curious enough to try things out with other team members.The structure of the organization must be carefully defined. The existing structure should present no complications. For example, it should not be difficult for the project manager to make decisions without consulting managers. The consultation process will drag the company down. A hierarchical structure may seem appealing, but it actually slows you down.The agile project management process is not complete without the use of agile tools. These are tools designed to help you work efficiently. The importance of using these tools is that you have time to focus on what's most important in the development process. Remember that you need to work fast and adapt quickly to changes. This may not bepossible if you follow the manual way. Forget the idea of using paperwork to keep track of things. There are many software products designed to automate the whole process. You better know the right tool for you.Popular agile tools you may come across during your research include Clarizen, Trello, Jira, Taiga, and Pivotal Tracker. Before choosing a tool, remember to browse its features. You can also test the product using the trial period. Don't pay for a product that tests its functionality.Yes, there are challenges you will encounter when implementing the agile method. However, you should always keep the bigger picture in mind and consider the many benefits that come with it. The agile method of project management always helps you to easily identify the wrong approaches. And last but not least, the method promotes quick decision making. This is made possible by the collaborative environment in which your team works. Keep in mind that an agile environment also fosters a culture that embraces change. Individuals come to understand that change is what makes the final product thrive on the market. This change will also likely make people flexible enough to quickly adapt to market needs.In addition, the project manager must not forget to measure the performance of his agile systems. This is the best way to continuously improve. The level of performance can be judged by the quality of the product. The final product they deliver to consumers must meet all of the expected requirements. In addition to delivering a quality product, on-time delivery is essential. Therefore, their success can also be measured by whether or not they completed the product ahead of schedule. Other ways to measure success include examining theProduct reach, project visibility and overall business value achieved through the use of an agile system.The agile project management method is quite convincing. There are many reasons to opt for the agile method. Forget the conventional way of doing things. Consumers today change their minds in an instant. Therefore, you need to be ready to quickly adapt to such changes. Keep in mind that your ability to change will greatly contribute to the success of your product. Determine the type of product you sell. Of course, a product suitable for all customer requirements will also have a high probability of performing well. Therefore, changing the way you manage projects makes a lot of sense. The agile method leads your organization to success.A lot of chance!

www.ingramcontent.com/pod-product-compliance
Lightning Source LLC
LaVergne TN
LVHW022058200926
848481LV00003B/980

* 9 7 8 1 8 0 4 7 7 2 6 7 6 *